For

The
LITTLE
BOOK
Of
Famous
INSULTS

COMPILED BY
SUSAN TELTSER-SCHWARZ

PETER PAUPER PRESS, INC.
WHITE PLAINS · NEW YORK

Copyright © 1993
Peter Pauper Press, Inc.
202 Mamaroneck Avenue
White Plains, NY 10601
All rights reserved
ISBN 0-88088-366-9
Printed in Hong Kong
7   6   5   4   3   2   1

THE LITTLE BOOK
OF FAMOUS INSULTS

He has Van Gogh's ear for music.
> *ORSON WELLES,*
> on Donny Osmond

Gerry Ford is a nice guy, but he played too much football with his helmet off.
> *LYNDON B. JOHNSON*

JOHN WILKES: I predict, sir, that you will die by hanging, or from some loathsome disease.

EARL OF SANDWICH: That depends, my dear sir, on whether I embrace your principles or your mistress!

Bernard Shaw had discovered himself
and gave ungrudgingly of his discovery
to the world.

H. H. MUNRO (SAKI)

They never open their mouths without subtracting from the sum of human knowledge.

THOMAS REED,
Speaker of the House,
about Congressmen

His body went to his head.

DOROTHY PARKER,
of drama critic John McClain,
who was vain about his build

He has achieved a political break-through—the Teflon-coated presidency. He sees to it that nothing sticks to him.

CONGRESSWOMAN PAT SCHROEDER,
on President Reagan

One-third mush and two-thirds Eleanor.

ALICE ROOSEVELT LONGWORTH,
on Franklin D. Roosevelt

Huh! And you're Required Reading!
COLLEGE GIRL,
on observing poet Louis Untermeyer
at a New Year's Eve party,
topped with paper hat
and blowing a horn

DOCTOR FRIEND OF CLARENCE DARROW:
I don't say lawyers are crooks, but you
must admit that the profession doesn't
exactly make angels of men.

CLARENCE DARROW: No, you doctors
have the better of us there.

A husband is what is left of the lover
after the nerve has been extracted.
                              HELEN ROWLAND

When Billy Martin reaches for a bar
tab, his arm shrinks six inches.
                              TOMMY LASORDA

[Charlie] Finley is a self-made man
who worships his creator.
                              JIM MURRAY

Nancy Reagan fell down and broke her hair.

JOHNNY CARSON

Tonstant Weader fwowed up.

DOROTHY PARKER,
reviewing *The House at Pooh Corner*

Forty years of romance make a woman
look like a ruin and forty years of
marriage make her look like a public
building.

OSCAR WILDE

I am willing to love all mankind,
except an American.

SAMUEL JOHNSON

Auctioneer, n. The man who proclaims
with a hammer that he has picked a
pocket with his tongue.

AMBROSE BIERCE

If a traveler were informed that such a man was leader of the House of Commons, he may well begin to comprehend how the Egyptians worshiped an insect.

BENJAMIN DISRAELI,
on Lord John Russell

Dan Quayle seems to be doing his job—making Bush look smart and presidential by comparison.

ANITA KATZ

Yes, but mine speaks English.

GOLDA MEIR,
about Henry Kissinger,
after President Nixon remarked that
both Israel and the United States had
Jewish foreign ministers

Literature is printed nonsense.

AUGUST STRINDBERG

He's the greatest husband in the world and he's nothing to brag about.

MARLO THOMAS,
about her husband, Phil Donahue

He speaks to me as if I were a public meeting.

QUEEN VICTORIA,
of William Gladstone

He's certain to get the divorce vote and remember that's one in four these days.

CLEVELAND AMORY,
on Nelson Rockefeller after his divorce

He's turned his life around. He used to be depressed and miserable. Now he's miserable and depressed.

HARRY KALAS,
about center fielder Garry Maddox

. . . Rhetoric that rolls like a freight train over a bridge.

DAVID BRINKLEY,
on John L. Lewis

For every year that you stay in California, you lose two points off your I.Q.

JAY PRESSON ALLEN,
Tru

No, madame, it's an error.

FATHER MUGNIER,
replying to a plump actress
who asked if it was a sin to look
at herself naked in a mirror

The House of Lords is the British
Outer Mongolia for retired politicians.
ANTHONY WEDGWOOD BENN

There's less here than meets the eye.
TALLULAH BANKHEAD,
about a Maeterlinck play

Consul, n. In American politics, a
person who having failed to secure an
office from the people is given one by
the Administration on condition that
he leave the country.
AMBROSE BIERCE

He looks as if he had been weaned on
a pickle.
ALICE ROOSEVELT LONGWORTH,
of Calvin Coolidge

I'm as pure as the driven slush.
TALLULAH BANKHEAD

Clarence Darrow was scheduled to speak in Chicago on "Why I am an Agnostic." He was approached by a reporter from the Chicago Tribune, who explained that he had an early edition to make and would be very grateful if Mr. Darrow could give him a prepared copy of the speech. Without looking up, Darrow reached into his pocket and handed the cub a blank pad of paper. "But Mr. Darrow," protested the reporter after a quick look, "this is the same speech you made last week."

He is a sheep in sheep's clothing.
WINSTON CHURCHILL,
on Clement Attlee

If Gladstone fell into the Thames, it would be a misfortune. But if someone dragged him out again, it would be a calamity.
BENJAMIN DISRAELI,
on the difference between
a misfortune and a calamity

The closest sound to Roseanne Barr's singing the National Anthem was my cat being neutered.

JOHNNY CARSON

I must decline your invitation owing to a subsequent engagement.

OSCAR WILDE

DOWAGER AT A BENEFIT AFFAIR: Oh, Mr. Shaw, what made you ask poor little me to dance?

GEORGE BERNARD SHAW: This is a charity ball, isn't it?

Certainly he is not of the generation that regards honesty as the best policy. However, he does regard it as a policy.

WALTER LIPPMANN,
on Richard Nixon

OSCAR WILDE: Oh, I wish I'd said that!

JAMES WHISTLER: You will, Oscar, you will.

I think he's for the birds, if that's what
you mean.

> *ROBERT REDFORD,*
> of George Bush as
> the environmental president

Frank Lorenzo demolished Eastern Airlines, wreaked havoc on thousands of workers' lives and severely devalued Continental Airlines. Our condolences to whatever industry he stalks next.

JOHN PETERPAUL,
union vice president

She has a history, but no past.

BARBARA CARTLAND,
on Princess Diana

RUTH GORDON: There's no scenery at all. In the first scene, I'm on the left side of the stage and the audience has to imagine I'm eating dinner in a restaurant. Then in scene two, I run over to the right side of the stage, and the audience imagines I'm in my drawing room.

GEORGE S. KAUFMAN: And the second night, *you* have to imagine there's an audience out front.

On the Vanna White diet, you only eat what you can spell.

JOAN RIVERS

The work of a queasy undergraduate
scratching his pimples.

VIRGINIA WOOLF,
on James Joyce's *Ulysses*

SAMUEL TAYLOR COLERIDGE: Did you
ever hear me preach?

CHARLES LAMB: I never heard you do
anything else.

He looked at foreign affairs through
the wrong end of a municipal
drainpipe.

WINSTON CHURCHILL,
of Neville Chamberlain

He hasn't an enemy in the world, and
none of his friends like him.

OSCAR WILDE,
of George Bernard Shaw

His mind is so open that the wind
whistles through it.

HEYWOOD BROUN,
of an impartial radio commentator

She is descended from a long line that
her mother listened to.

> *GYPSY ROSE LEE,*
> on a pretentious chorus girl

He can't see a belt without hitting
below it.

> *MARGOT ASQUITH,*
> on Lloyd George

Hook and Ladder is the sort of play that
gives failures a bad name.

> *WALTER KERR*

The trouble with you, Lennox, is that
when you're not drunk, you're sober.

> *WILLIAM BUTLER YEATS,*
> on Lennox Robinson

Play Hemingway. Be fierce.

GERTRUDE STEIN,
to her dog

Hemingway, remarks are not literature.
GERTRUDE STEIN

Politics is perhaps the only profession for which no preparation is thought necessary.
ROBERT LOUIS STEVENSON

Tell me, George, if you had to do it all over, would you fall in love with yourself again?

OSCAR LEVANT,
to George Gershwin

GEORGE BERNARD SHAW (to his wife, in an argument with someone else): Isn't it true, my dear, that male judgment is superior to female judgment?

MRS. SHAW: Of course, dear. After all, you married me and I you.

His forehead was so wrinkled, he had
to screw his hat on.

CARLETON ALSOP

That's not writing, that's typing.

TRUMAN CAPOTE,
on Jack Kerouac, who boasted of
never rereading a manuscript
after having written it

You can't make the Duchess into
Rebecca of Sunnybrook Farm.

CLEVELAND AMORY,
on why he stopped helping
the Duchess of Windsor
write her memoirs

Ask him the time and he'll tell you
how the watch was made.

JANE WYMAN,
on her former husband,
Ronald Reagan

If a man stay away from his wife for
seven years, the law presumes the
separation to have killed him; yet,
according to our daily experience, it
might well prolong his life.

C. J. DARLING

Claude Debussy played the piano with the lid down.

ROBERT BRESSON

You must have taken great pains, sir;
you could not naturally have been so
very stupid.

SAMUEL JOHNSON

Anoint, v.t. To grease a king or other
great functionary already sufficiently
slippery.

AMBROSE BIERCE

A healthy male adult bore consumes
each year one and a half times his own
weight in other people's patience.

JOHN UPDIKE

Mr. Joseph Chamberlain likes the
working classes; he likes to watch them
work.

WINSTON CHURCHILL

Lawrence of Arabia was standing on the porch of a Cairo hotel one hot morning when he was approached by a lady celebrity-stalker. "Imagine, Colonel Lawrence," she bubbled, fluttering her fan. "Ninety-two already!"

"Indeed!" replied the colonel with a bow. "Many happy returns of the day!"

The way Bernard Shaw believes in himself is very refreshing in these atheistic days when so many people believe in no God at all.

ISRAEL ZANGWILL

ARTHUR MURRAY (about an actress): She's her own worst enemy.

GROUCHO MARX: Not while I'm alive, she isn't.

Some American delusions:
1. That there is no class-consciousness in the country.
2. That American coffee is good.
3. That Americans are businesslike.
4. That Americans are highly sexed and that redheads are more highly sexed than others.

W. SOMERSET MAUGHAM

Madonna shaved her legs to lose 30 pounds.

JOAN RIVERS

Baldwin occasionally stumbles over the truth, but he always hastily picks himself up and hurries on as if nothing had happened.

WINSTON CHURCHILL

Katharine Hepburn (in *The Lake*) runs the gamut of emotions from A to B.

DOROTHY PARKER

An empty cab drove up, and Sarah Bernhardt got out.

ARTHUR "BUGS" BAER

A day away from Tallulah is like a month in the country.

ANONYMOUS

It was very good of God to let Carlyle and Mrs. Carlyle marry one another and so make only two people miserable instead of four.

SAMUEL BUTLER

It's redundant to die in California.
                            JAY PRESSON ALLEN,
                                              Tru

Alliance, n. In international politics,
the union of two thieves who have
their hands so deeply inserted in each
other's pocket that they cannot
separately plunder a third.
                            AMBROSE BIERCE

All tragedies are finish'd by a death,
    All comedies are ended by a marriage.
                            LORD BYRON

When President Woodrow Wilson
became seriously ill in office, his wife
took over his functions to such a
degree that she was called *Acting First
Man* and her period of power *Mrs.
Wilson's Regency.*

Dewey has thrown his diaper into the ring.

HAROLD L. ICKES

Is she fat? Her favorite food is seconds.

JOAN RIVERS,
of Elizabeth Taylor

No one ever went broke under-
estimating the taste of the American
public.

H. L. MENCKEN

Television is called a medium because
it is neither rare nor well done.

ERNIE KOVACS

It was a bad play saved by a bad
performance.

GEORGE S. KAUFMAN,
about *Skylark,*
starring Gertrude Lawrence

Now at least I know where he is!
                    QUEEN ALEXANDRA,
            on hearing of the death of her
                    husband, Edward VII,
            who was notoriously unfaithful

A fifty-year trespass against good taste.

LESLIE MALLORY,
about the life of Errol Flynn

It's great to be with Bill Buckley, because you don't have to think. He takes a position and you automatically take the opposite one and you know you're right.

JOHN KENNETH GALBRAITH

Macaulay has occasional flashes of silence that make his conversation perfectly delightful.

SYDNEY SMITH

According to the Bible, woman was the last thing God made. It must have been a Saturday night. Clearly, He was tired.

ALEXANDRE DUMAS, FILS

Princess Di wears more clothes in one
day than Gandhi wore in his entire life.
JOAN RIVERS

In the first place God made idiots; this was for practice; then he made school boards.

MARK TWAIN

A baby is an alimentary canal with a loud voice at one end and no responsibility at the other.

E. ADAMSON

Marriage always demands the greatest understanding of the art of insincerity possible between two human beings.

VICKI BAUM

He has sat so long upon the fence that the iron has entered into his soul.

LLOYD GEORGE,
of Sir John Simon

A triumph of the embalmer's art.

GORE VIDAL,
about Ronald Reagan

He has been called a mediocre man; but this is unwarranted flattery. He was a politician of monumental littleness.

THEODORE ROOSEVELT,
of President John Tyler

Mike Anderson's limitations are limitless.

DANNY OZARK,
on a Phillies outfielder

He who can, does. He who cannot, teaches.

GEORGE BERNARD SHAW

You're obviously suffering from delusions of adequacy.

ALEXIS CARRINGTON,
character in soap opera *Dynasty*

ACTOR: I've never been better! In the last act yesterday, I had the audience glued to their seats.

OLIVER HERFORD: How clever of you to think of it!

What could Adam have done to God
that made Him put Eve in the garden?
POLISH PROVERB

Leo Durocher is a man with an infinite
capacity for immediately making a bad
thing worse.

BRANCH RICKEY

How can they tell?

DOROTHY PARKER,
on learning that
Calvin Coolidge was dead

Nowadays, another place where men
aren't safe from women drivers is a
golf course.

JOE E. BROWN

MAN WHO LOST AN ARGUMENT TO CHURCHMAN SYDNEY SMITH: If I had a son who was an idiot, I would make him a parson.

SYDNEY SMITH: Your father was of a different opinion.

How thrilling it would be, if only one couldn't read!

> *G. K. CHESTERTON,*
> on first seeing Times Square at night

When you get home, throw your mother a bone.

> *DOROTHY PARKER*

Tallulah Bankhead barged down the Nile last night as Cleopatra—and sank.

> *JOHN MASON BROWN*

The covers of this book are too far apart.

> *AMBROSE BIERCE*

Prince Charles's ears are so big he could hang-glide over the Falklands.

JOAN RIVERS

I wish you'd kept your hair and lost
the rest of you.

line from the
Dick Van Dyke show

The trouble with lawyers is that they
are insufferable word stretchers.

NERO WOLFE

He's a taker, boring, and insincere, but
outside of that, I like him!

ARTHUR L. SCHWARZ

She must sharpen her tongue on
barbed wire.

CHARLOTTE ROSENTHAL

If brains was lard, Jethro couldn't
grease a pan.

JED CLAMPETT,
character on *The Beverly Hillbillies*

She's two-faced, and in her case one is more than enough.

SUSAN TELTSER-SCHWARZ

Mayor Dinkins is a good example of unskilled labor.

MURRAY GOLDSTEIN,
a New York City taxpayer

Gout, n. A physician's name for the rheumatism of a rich patient.

AMBROSE BIERCE

Mr. Depew says that if you open my mouth and drop in a dinner, up will come a speech. But I warn you that, if you open your mouths and drop in one of Mr. Depew's speeches, up will come your dinners.

AMBASSADOR JOSEPH H. CHOATE

He was like a cock who thought the sun had risen to hear him crow.

GEORGE ELIOT

Such an active lass. So outdoorsy. She loves nature in spite of what it did to her.

> *BETTE MIDLER,*
> about Princess Anne

A man with your low intelligence should have a voice to match.

> *LORD MANCROFT,*
> to a loud-voiced heckler

When men reach middle age, they get sadder and wiser; when women do, they get sadder and wider.

> *EVAN ESAR*

It is not true that I said actors are cattle. I said they should be *treated* like cattle.

> *ALFRED HITCHCOCK*

Here lies my wife: here let her lie!
Now she's at rest, and so am I.

JOHN DRYDEN,
epitaph for his wife

Lawyer, n. One skilled in circumvention of the law.

AMBROSE BIERCE

He (Napoleon III) is a great unrecognized incapacity.

OTTO VON BISMARCK

I looked into those blue eyes, and I might as well have been looking out the window.

WILLIAM CAVANAUGH,
college professor of Dan Quayle

[Richard Nixon has] the integrity of a hyena and the style of a poison toad.

HUNTER S. THOMPSON

Wagner's music is better than it
sounds.

MARK TWAIN

An ego that can crack crystal at a distance of twenty feet.

> *JOHN CHEEVER,*
> of Yevtushenko

I am watching your performance from the rear of the house. Wish you were here.

> *GEORGE S. KAUFMAN,*
> telegram to an actor
> performing in one of his plays

Alfred Lunt has his head in the clouds and his feet in the box office.

> *NOEL COWARD*

Senate, n. A body of elderly gentlemen charged with high duties and misdemeanors.

> *AMBROSE BIERCE*

NO. 1 2 3 4 5 6 7 8 – A.B.C
BORN U.S.A
RES. 97 SNOOP ST.

If you actually look like your passport
photo, you aren't well enough to travel.
SIR VIVIAN FUCHS

Those without sin shall stone the first cast.

WALTER WINCHELL,
after seeing a bad
performance of a new show

The Irish are a fair people—they never speak well of one another.

SAMUEL JOHNSON

Senator, I served with Jack Kennedy. I knew Jack Kennedy. Jack Kennedy was a friend of mine. Senator, you're no Jack Kennedy.

LLOYD BENTSEN,
on Dan Quayle, who compared
himself to Jack Kennedy

Last weekend I went to Philadelphia but it was closed.

W. C. FIELDS

The most happy marriage I can picture . . . would be the union of a deaf man to a blind woman.

SAMUEL COLERIDGE